STATES OF MATTER

BY MARY GRIFFIN

Gareth Stevens
PUBLISHING

CRASHCOURSE

Please visit our website, www.garethstevens.com. For a free color catalog of all our high-quality books, call toll free 1-800-542-2595 or fax 1-877-542-2596.

Library of Congress Cataloging-in-Publication Data

Names: Griffin, Mary, 1978- author.
Title: States of matter / Mary Griffin.
Description: New York : Gareth Stevens Publishing, [2019] | Series: A look at chemistry | Includes index.
Identifiers: LCCN 2018016719| ISBN 9781538230138 (library bound) | ISBN 9781538231630 (pbk.) | ISBN 9781538233306 (6 pack)
Subjects: LCSH: Matter--Properties--Juvenile literature.
Classification: LCC QC173.16 .G75 2019 | DDC 530.4--dc23
LC record available at https://lccn.loc.gov/2018016719

First Edition

Published in 2019 by
Gareth Stevens Publishing
111 East 14th Street, Suite 349
New York, NY 10003

Copyright © 2019 Gareth Stevens Publishing

Designer: Reann Nye
Editor: Therese Shea

Photo credits: Series art Marina Sun/Shutterstock.com; cover Mark Scott/Shutterstock.com; p. 5 wundervisuals/E+/Getty Images; p. 7 (top) Valentyn Volkov/Shutterstock.com; p. 7 (middle) khak/Shutterstock.com; p. 7 (bottom) Africa Studio/Shutterstock.com; p. 9 isak55/Shutterstock.com; p. 17 Shark_749/Shutterstock.com; p. 19 jakkapan/ Shutterstock.com; p. 21 Dmitry Kovba/Shutterstock.com; p. 25 Tom Begasse/ Shutterstock.com; p. 27 David Skulich/Shutterstock.com; p. 29 Hero Images/Getty Images.

Printed in the United States of America

CPSIA compliance information: Batch #CW19GS: For further information contact Gareth Stevens, New York, New York at 1-800-542-2595.

CONTENTS

Words in the glossary appear in **bold** type the first time they are used in the text.

MATTER MATTERS

Look around you. All you can see—and can't see—is matter. Matter is everything that takes up space. That includes anything you touch as well as the gases that make up the air we breathe.

MAKE THE GRADE

All matter has mass, even gases!

5

Matter is found in three main forms, or phases. They are solid, liquid, and gas. You see these forms every day in water. Liquid water can turn into solid ice. Water also takes a gas form called water vapor. You can't see water vapor.

SOLID

LIQUID

MAKE THE GRADE

When water boils, it turns into steam. You can see "wet steam," which has drops of liquid water mixed with water vapor.

GAS

ATOMS AND MOLECULES

What happens to matter that causes its form to change? To understand this, you must understand what matter is made of—atoms. Atoms are the smallest bits of matter. An element is a **substance** made from just one kind of atom.

MAKE THE GRADE

There are 118 known kinds of elements—which means there are 118 kinds of atoms!

Atoms of an element **chemically** combine to make groups called molecules. Molecules can be countless sizes and shapes. They form the different kinds of matter. But molecules are always in motion. The atoms within them turn and shake, too!

VITAMIN C COMPOUND

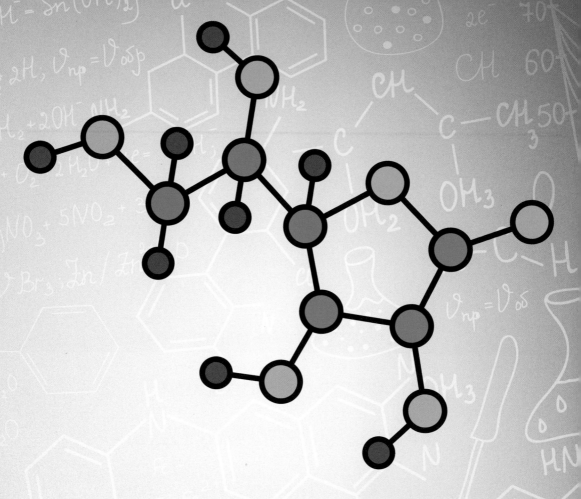

⬤ CARBON ⬤ OXYGEN ⬤ HYDROGEN

 MAKE THE GRADE

Molecules with more than one kind of element are often called compounds.

Where an atom is placed in a molecule, how it's moving, and the strength of its attraction to other atoms can change. Temperature and pressure are two **factors** that can cause change. They can cause the state of matter to change, too.

OXYGEN GAS (O₂)

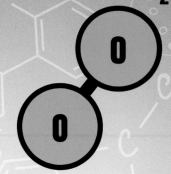

CARBON DIOXIDE
(CO₂)

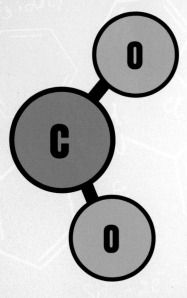

METHANE
(CH₄)

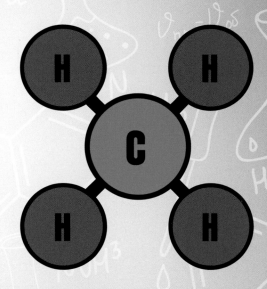

MAKE THE GRADE

Elements are often marked as a letter in models of molecules. For example, "H" means hydrogen, "O" means oxygen, and "C" means carbon.

SOLIDS, LIQUIDS, GASES

Under ordinary conditions, 2 elements are liquid, 11 are gases, and the rest are solids. In solid matter, molecules are packed tightly together. They have a strong **attraction** to each other. That's why solids hold a certain shape.

CRYSTALLINE SOLID

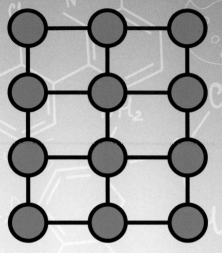

AMORPHOUS SOLID

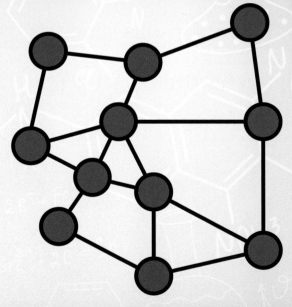

MAKE THE GRADE

A crystalline solid has atoms or molecules arranged in a regular pattern. Other solids aren't as ordered. They're called amorphous solids.

There's always some space between molecules in a solid. In a liquid, molecules have even more space between them. They're attracted to each other but can move around. That's why liquids can be poured. Liquids take the shape of the container they fill.

MAKE THE GRADE

A liquid's **volume** doesn't change, no matter what container it's in.

Gas molecules are even farther apart than liquid molecules. They're not close enough to be attracted to each other. They move at high speeds. A gas will **expand** and fill any container. Gases can also be **compressed** to take up less volume.

MAKE THE GRADE

A gas's volume changes with the volume of its container! Helium is a gas used to blow up balloons and make them float.

CHANGING STATES

Matter may change states when a condition around it changes. Let's see how a change in temperature affects the molecules of water. Water is the only matter in nature found in gas, liquid, and solid form on our planet.

MAKE THE GRADE

Scientists have found ways to make matter other than water change states. In fact, all elements can exist as solids, liquids, and gases!

Rising temperatures cause molecules in liquid water to move around more. If the temperature is high enough, the liquid changes into a hot gas called steam. If the temperature becomes cold enough, molecules in liquid water slow and attract. Water becomes a solid—ice!

GAS

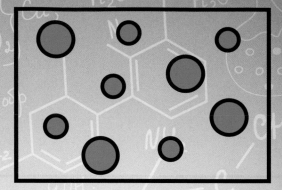

HOT

LIQUID

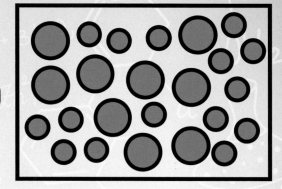

SOLID

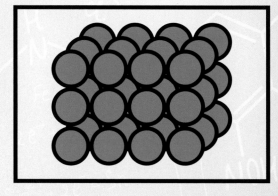

COLD

MAKE THE GRADE

Ice can become a gas without turning into a liquid first. This is called sublimation.

23

Pressure can also affect states of matter. Pressure from Earth's **atmosphere** is greater in the mountains than at sea level. In the mountains, water boils—and changes into steam—at a higher temperature than at sea level!

MAKE THE GRADE

Great pressure deep within Earth
causes solids to become liquids!

25

OTHER STATES OF MATTER

Plasma is a state of matter, too. It occurs at very hot temperatures. In plasmas, atoms move around so much they knock bits called electrons away from atoms' **nuclei**. Neon gas becomes plasma when heated with electricity. It's used to make signs glow!

ATOM

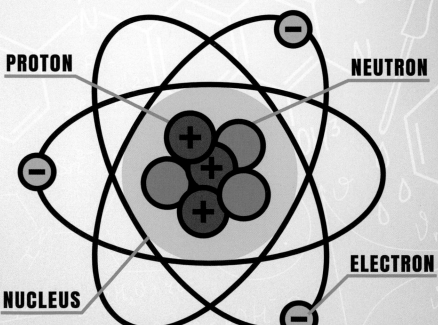

PROTON

NEUTRON

ELECTRON

NUCLEUS

Bose-Einstein condensates are a state of matter first created in a lab in the 1990s. In this state, atoms are cooled to almost **absolute zero** until they hardly move. Still other states of matter are just **theories**! Will you prove they're true?

MAKE THE GRADE

Even when the state of matter changes, its chemical **properties** don't change. It's still the same matter!

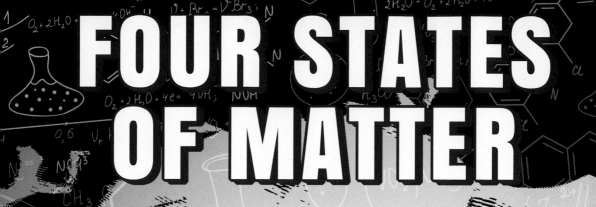

FOUR STATES OF MATTER

ADDING ENERGY (HEATING) →

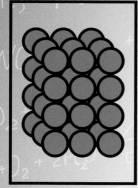 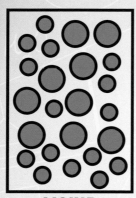 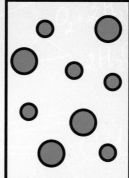 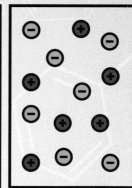

| **SOLID** | **LIQUID** | **GAS** | **PLASMA** |
| (strong bond) | (weak bond) | (no bond) | |

← **REMOVING ENERGY (COOLING)**

⬤ **ATOM**

⊕ **NUCLEUS**

⊖ **ELECTRON**

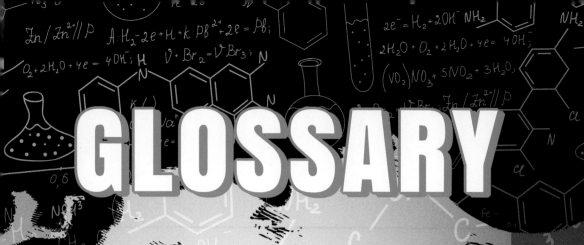

GLOSSARY

absolute zero: the temperature believed to be the lowest possible temperature. It's about $-459.67°F$ ($-273.15°C$).

atmosphere: the mixture of gases that surround a planet

attraction: a force that pulls something to or toward something else

chemically: in a way that uses chemicals. A chemical is matter that can be mixed with other matter to cause changes.

compress: to press or squeeze together

expand: to get larger and looser

factor: one of the things that cause something to happen

nucleus: the central part of an atom that is made up of protons and neutrons. The plural of nucleus is nuclei.

property: a special quality or feature of something

substance: a certain kind of matter

theory: an explanation based on facts that is generally accepted by scientists

volume: the amount of space an object takes up

universe: everything that exists

FOR MORE INFORMATION

BOOKS

Deschermeier, Charlotte. *Different States of Matter*. New York, NY: PowerKids Press, 2014.

James, Emily. *The Simple Science of Matter*. North Mankato, MN: Capstone Press, 2018.

Kenney, Karen Latchana. *States of Matter Investigations*. Minneapolis, MN: Lerner Publications, 2018.

WEBSITES

States of Matter
www.chem4kids.com/files/matter_states.html
Read more about the states of matter.

Molecules
www.sciencekids.co.nz/gamesactivities/detectivescience/statesof matter.html
Solve a mystery about the states of matter!

Publisher's note to educators and parents: Our editors have carefully reviewed these websites to ensure that they are suitable for students. Many websites change frequently, however, and we cannot guarantee that a site's future contents will continue to meet our high standards of quality and educational value. Be advised that students should be closely supervised whenever they access the internet.

INDEX

DATE DUE

PRINTED IN U.S.A.